The Prayer Practice

Practicing the Way

Welcome

Welcome to the Prayer Practice. You may have joined this Practice because you're new to following Jesus and learning to pray for the very first time. Or you may be at a stage in your apprenticeship to Jesus where you desire to not just learn about God, but to *experience* God. Or you may just find prayer boring or tedious, but you have a growing sense there's something you've yet to discover.

Whatever your motivation, we're so happy you've chosen to go on this four-week journey into a deeper life with God. In the hurry, distraction, and noise of the modern world, few things are more difficult, or more rewarding, than developing a life of prayer.

Prayer is simply the medium through which we communicate and commune with God. The practice of prayer is learning to set aside dedicated time to intentionally be with God, in order to become like him and partner with him in the world.

Over the next four weeks, the plan is to explore four stages of prayer.

01   Talking to God
02   Talking with God
03   Listening to God
04   Being with God

You can think of these four stages of prayer as *layers* by which we go deeper with God. When you are first learning to pray, there is a bit of a progression from one stage to the next. But the spiritual journey is not a linear progression, and you never mature beyond any dimension of prayer.

As you give yourself to Jesus through this Practice, please remember: The ultimate aim is not to "pray more" or "pray better". It's what ancient Christians called union with God. As Julian of Norwich said long ago, "The whole reason why we pray is to be *united* into the vision and contemplation of him to whom we pray." It's to live each day more and more aware of and deeply connected to our Father; to be transformed into the likeness of his Son, Jesus; and to be filled with the fullness of his Spirit, to do what he made you to do in the world.

Table of Contents

Tips

This Companion Guide is full of spiritual exercises, best practices, and good advice on how to pray. But it's important to note at the top prayer is not a technique that, if we learn, can somehow control our life with God. It's a way of setting ourselves before God, not to control our relationship with him, but to surrender to his love.

The goal isn't to "get good" at prayer, but to create new daily rhythms and ways of being that open us to God's goodness in more profound ways.

It's so easy to lose sight of the ultimate aim of a Practice; here are a few tips to keep in mind as you pray.

01   Start small

Start where you *are*, not where you "should be". If 30 minutes a day is too much, start with 10. If daily is too much, start with weekly.

02   Think subtraction, not addition

Please do not add a daily prayer rhythm into your already overbusy, overfull life. Think, "What can I cut out?" A morning glance at the news? A lunch break scroll through social media? An evening TV show habit? Formation is about less, not more.

03   You get out what you put in

The more fully you give yourself to this Practice, the more life-changing it will be. The more you just dabble with it, the more shortcuts you take, the less of an effect it will have on your transformation.

04   Remember the J-curve

Experts on learning tell us that mastering a new skill tends to follow a J-shaped curve; we tend to get worse before we get better. If you currently enjoy your times of prayer, don't be surprised if some of these new types of prayer feel awkward and difficult. Just stay with the Practice; you will come around.

05   There is no formation without repetition

Spiritual formation is slow, deep, cumulative work that takes years, not weeks. The goal of this four-week experience is just to get you started on a journey of a lifetime. Upon completion of this Practice, you will have a map for the journey ahead and hopefully some possible companions for the Way. But what you do next is up to you.

A note about the Reach Exercise

We recognize that we're all at different places in our stage of discipleship and season of life. To that end, we've added a Reach Exercise to each of the four weeks if you want to go further in prayer. For each Reach Exercise, you'll find written instructions and a companion video tutorial (via QR code).

The Prayer Reach Exercises were written in collaboration with Strahan Coleman, a musician, writer, retreat leader, and spiritual director from Aotearoa, the Māori name for New Zealand, and a contributor to Practicing the Way. You can find more of his work at commonerscommunion.com.

Additionally, we have weekly readings and corresponding episodes from the Rule of Life podcast to enhance all four sessions. Enjoy!

A note about the recommended reading

Reading a book alongside the Practice can greatly enhance your understanding and enjoyment of prayer. You may love to read, or you may not. For that reason, it's recommended, but certainly not required.

Our companion book for the Prayer Practice is *Praying Like Monks, Living Like Fools* by Tyler Staton, who is the lead pastor of Bridgetown Church in Portland, Oregon, and the national director of 24-7 Prayer USA.

May Jesus teach you to pray — to commune and communicate with our Father — and lead you into a deeper life of union with the Spirit.

Talking to God

WEEK 01

Overview

In Week 01, we explore the first stage of prayer: talking to God. When the disciples asked Jesus, "Teach us to pray," in Luke 11, Jesus replied, "This, then, is how you should pray: "'Our Father in heaven, hallowed be your name...'" He gave them a pre-made prayer, or what some call a liturgy, to pray to God.

Liturgies can look like praying the Lord's Prayer, singing through the Psalms or using a prayer app on your phone. This way of praying can be incredibly helpful in various seasons of our lives: when we're learning to pray, when we're exhausted or sick, when we're traveling and find it hard to focus, or when we're living with grief and doubt, searching for the right words to talk to God. "The prayers of the saints," as some call them, can carry us through.

So we start our four-week journey simply, by praying pre-made prayers to God.

This week's Practice will focus on the pragmatics of prayer. One of the single most important tasks of discipleship to Jesus is starting, habituating, and fine-tuning a daily prayer rhythm. Your daily prayer can be simple and brief. And as essential as sleeping, eating, and drinking. This is what will keep you praying in the days, months, and years to come.

Ronald Rolheiser writes:

> "What clear, simple, and brief rituals provide is precisely prayer that depends upon something beyond our own energy. The rituals carry us, our tiredness, our lack of energy, our inattentiveness, our indifference, and even our occasional distaste. They keep us praying even when we are too tired to muster up our own energy."

Here are a few questions to hold in your mind as we enter this week's Practice.

When will I pray? First thing in the morning? After my workout? At night? On my lunch break? When the kids are napping? Many people find first thing in the morning to be best, but not always. As a general rule, give God your best time of day, when you are most awake and aware.

Where will I pray? Most of us find it incredibly helpful to choose a dedicated space for prayer — a room in our home, a corner in our bedroom, a park bench near our house, or a literal prayer closet. This place can become a kind of modern day altar, where you go to open to God. Not because God hears us better at an altar, but because we hear God better!

How should I pray? What posture is best for me? Sitting on a chair, a couch, or the floor? Kneeling? Standing? Walking? Lying down? Out loud or quiet? Does it help to begin with deep breathing first? How do I get my body to work with my heart's desire for God, not against it?

How long should I pray? There's no "right" answer (to this or any of the other questions), but as a general rule: long enough to become present to God. And that may take a bit longer than you expect. If you have a newborn child or some other extenuating circumstances that make 30 minutes too hard, that's fine. Start where you are and take the next step forward in your journey.

In general, if we can't pray for 30 minutes a day, we're simply too busy. And we need to take a serious life audit of what we believe is most important to us. After all, we're not trying to layer on more Christian busyness to our already over-maxed lives; we're trying to slow down and simplify our lives around what we most deeply desire — God.

Practice

01   Create a daily prayer rhythm

Decide on a time and a place to pray, if possible, every day this week.

Decide on and commit to a time duration. Don't overreach. Start where you are. If you don't pray daily, aim for 10-15 minutes. If you pray for 10-15 minutes, consider upping it to half an hour. Just take the next step.

Create routines or rituals you actually enjoy to make your daily prayer habit something you look forward to all day long — light a candle, make yourself coffee or tea, sit by a window you love, go outside, savor the quiet, or put on worship music.

Those of you who are more kinesthetic may find it helpful to pray while walking, inside or in nature, or with something to keep your hands busy, like knitting or drawing.

Ultimately, work with your personality, not against it.

02 Pick out a pre-made prayer and talk to God

Try using one of the sources we mentioned earlier.

- **The Lord's Prayer**
- **The Psalms** — See below for recommendations
- **Scripture** — Find a passage that resonates with your heart and pray it back to God
- **Singing** — Sing acapella, put on a worship album, or play an instrument
- **Liturgy** — *The Book of Common Prayer*, *The Divine Hours* by Phyllis Tickle, or *Every Moment Holy* by Douglas Kaine McKelvey
- **Apps** — Lectio 365 from 24-7 Prayer, Pray as You Go from the Jesuits, or Hallow

If you don't have a strong preference, we recommend you start by praying the Psalms or one of the prayers in the Appendix of this Companion Guide.

You can start in Psalm 1 and pray through the book. Or you can pray a psalm based on your emotional or spiritual state that day.

Here are some recommendations.

- **To begin your day with God:** Psalm 5, 19, 20, 23, 25
- **When you are sad:** Psalm 13, 22, 42, 77
- **When you are in distress:** Psalm 57, 60, 86
- **When you are scared:** Psalm 27
- **When you are hurt:** Psalm 10
- **When you ache for more of God:** Psalm 63, 84
- **When you want to repent:** Psalm 51
- **When you are grateful:** Psalm 9, 103
- **When you want to worship:** Psalm 8, 148-150

Whatever you decide, pray at least once a day.

NOTES

Reach Practice

WEEK 01: TALKING TO GOD

Reading

Read chapters 1-3 of *Praying Like Monks, Living Like Fools* by Tyler Staton (pp. 1-68).

Podcast

Listen to episode 1 of the Prayer series from the Rule of Life podcast by Practicing the Way.

Exercise: Praying the Lord's Prayer

This week's Reach Exercise is to utilize the Lord's Prayer as a template for a longer time of prayer by praying through each line. This should take around 15 minutes to pray, but feel free to take it at your own pace, listening to the Spirit's prompting.

Note: You can do this exercise alone or as a group.

Follow the QR code above to a video tutorial from Strahan Coleman that will guide you step by step, using prayer prompts.

Or you can follow the written tutorial on the following pages.

NOTES

Reach Practice

WEEK 01: TALKING TO GOD

To begin, find somewhere quiet. Put away your phones or any other distractions, and get into a comfortable, but alert position.

Take a few deep, slow breaths. Become aware of your surroundings, the sounds, how your body is today. Open up to God in this present moment.

Then, praying from what you imagine or feel is a deep place within you, pray like this:

"Our Father"	Think about the idea of God as your loving Parent, one who has good and kind intentions toward you. If you like, imagine him embracing you, or smiling at you. Picture his face. Make eye contact with him.
"In heaven"	Think about the idea that God is all around you. Like oxygen, he surrounds and soaks your body, his Spirit abiding within you like oxygen. As you breathe, imagine that each breath invites God deeper into you, remembering that God loves living here, in you.

"Hallowed be your name"

Sit with your Father in joyful, grateful worship. You might want to sit in silence for a few moments. Or sing a chorus. Or rattle off a list of things you're grateful for. Or praise God with specific things you love about him. You may just want to imagine your whole being caught up into his, and what it feels like to be mingled with the God of love.

If you are in a group, encourage people to make their expressions of praise and gratitude out loud, one at a time. (E.g., "Father, thank you for your kindness." "Father, thank you for loving me.")

"Your kingdom come, your will be done, on earth as it is in heaven"

As we experience God's heart, allow it to inspire prayer for your city/church/community/life. Pray from this place of parental love. Allow the Spirit to lead you towards people, places, and situations that he longs to deliver, heal, and provide for. This type of prayer is referred to as intercession.

If you don't have a sense of God's leading, that's okay, think of specific things you're aware of in your life and others to pray for.

If you're in a group, one at a time, spend time as a group verbally giving to God specific things in your life that you're wrestling with control over. A simple prayer of, "Your will be done in _____ ," is a great place to start.

"Give us each day our daily bread"

Now spend some time asking God for things you need. Remembering that God is your Father, bring to him the provision, healing, and understanding you need, asking him to intervene. Your daily bread may be physical, relational, financial, emotional, or spiritual. Think of all the places you need him, inviting him to arrive there.

If you are in a group, do this with each person praying silently, out loud one at a time, or all together at once.

"Forgive us our debts, as we also have forgiven our debtors"

Knowing that God sees you and longs to heal every part of you, spend a few minutes now in quiet asking God for forgiveness in specific areas in your life. You can do that by speaking out loud the specific areas of sin and shame in your life, or by asking the Spirit to search your heart and reveal them to you.

Once you're done, ask the same for those who have sinned against you, asking the Spirit to help you to continue to forgive them, releasing them to God.

If you are in a group, break into groups of 2-3 to confess sin to each other, only as you feel comfortable, or sit in a few moments of silence together.

"And lead us not into temptation, but deliver us from evil"

Ask for God's strength and resolve to resist temptation in the three enemies of your soul: the World, the Flesh, and the Devil.

The World: its ideologies, consumerism and materialism, promiscuity, escapism, addiction, and greed. The Flesh: its pride, self-gratification, lust, and prejudice. The Devil: his lies, shaming, hatred, violence, and accusing.

Ask for the Spirit to save you from giving into the temptation of all three, even from what you're unable to see in your life. Ask for God's positive blessings in these spaces, inviting his goodness to lead the way and make itself evident in your every moment.

"For yours is the kingdom, the power and the glory, forever and ever. Amen"

Take a moment to verbally declare the reality of this in your own language. Attributing with love all glory to God in your body, your life, and the world around you.

Finish with a prayer of thankfulness and gratitude for God's presence with you during this time.

Prayer Reflection

WEEK 01: TALKING TO GOD

Reflection is a key component in our spiritual formation.

Millenia ago, King David prayed in Psalm 139v23-24:

> Search me, God, and know my heart;
>   test me and know my anxious thoughts.
> See if there is any offensive way in me,
>   and lead me in the way everlasting.

Trevor Hudson, a scholar on Ignatian spirituality, has said, "We don't change from our experience, we change when we reflect on our experience."

If you want to get the most out of this Practice, you need to do it and then *reflect* on it.

Before your next time together with the group for Week 02, take five to ten minutes to journal out your answers to the following three questions.

01 Where did I feel resistance?

02 Where did I feel delight?

03 Where did I most experience God's nearness?

Note: As you write, be as specific as possible. While bullet points are just fine, if you write it out in narrative form, your brain will be able to process your insights in a more lasting way.

Talking with God

WEEK 02

Overview

In Week 02, we begin to learn how to talk with God. Praying pre-made prayers is a beautiful way to pray. It's where we start our prayer journey, and it's a place we revisit all through our lives. But at some point in our life of prayer, we desire to pray our *own* words to God — to share what's on our mind, our heart. Our pain, our joy, our hopes and fears. We can't help but desire to interact with God in a more authentic, personalized way.

We break down this next stage of prayer into three subcategories.

01 **Gratitude** — talking with God about what is good in your life and world

02 **Lament** — talking with God about what is evil in your life and world

03 **Petition and Intercession** — asking God to fulfill his promises to overcome evil with good

Each one of these three dimensions of talking with God is like a vast territory we can explore for a lifetime and yet never see it all.

Practice

WEEK 02: TALKING WITH GOD

01 Fine tune your daily prayer rhythm

It can take a very long time to figure out your daily routine for prayer —
where to pray, when, how long, etc. And it's a moving target in the
different seasons of our lives. So we're always fine tuning; what's working,
what's not?

Here are two things to consider incorporating into what you started
last week.

- **Find an aid to "transition" in and out of prayer**
  - Think of this aid as a micro-ritual to begin and end your daily
    time. You could light a candle, sit in silence for a few minutes,
    take ten deep, slow breaths, go for a walk, or utilize music.
    It can be *anything* that helps you un-hurry and recenter on
    God's presence.
- **Use your body in prayer**
  - We have an embodied faith and a wandering mind, so
    posture matters a lot in prayer.
  - Biblically, the most common way to pray is not sitting or even
    kneeling, but standing up and lifting your hands. But you
    can also pray sitting on the floor, kneeling, lying face down,

walking, or, like Jesus did, climbing a mountain!

- ○ Different postures are more conducive to different types of prayer. For example, standing and lifting your hands is ideal for intercessory prayer. Kneeling or lying facedown on the floor are fitting postures for confession, repentance, or surrender. Walking can be a great posture to unburden your heart to God. Sitting cross legged on the floor or in a firm chair to aid deep breathing is very helpful for quiet, contemplative prayer. There's no "right" way. Just experiment with your body and your daily prayer rhythm.

02 Begin and/or end your day with gratitude

While there's no "right" way to practice gratitude, we encourage you to use your imagination and creativity to "give thanks in all circumstances," as written in 1 Thessalonians 5v18.

Here are a few ideas.

- Begin your daily prayer time by giving thanks for three gifts of the day.
- Give thanks during everyday moments like while you commute to work, take a shower, or walk your dog.
- Keep a gratitude journal.
- Write out three gratitudes on a small piece of paper each morning, and then carry them in your pocket all day long.
- Go around the table at dinner with your family, spouse, roommates, or community and say what you are thankful for.

However you do it, at *least* once a day, pause, and give thanks for at least three good things in your life.

03 Ask

Step into petition and intercession, and ask on behalf of yourself and others. We have two recommended exercises to do this.

- **Prayer Cards**
    - ○ Make a deck of index cards with names or situations at the top of each card (or you can do one card with the most important people and situations in your life). We challenge you to consider including your enemies or those you are struggling to forgive, as praying for them can set your heart free to love them.
    - ○ Flip through your cards and linger over each one for a few seconds to a few minutes, offering up specific prayers to our Father. Remember, generic prayers make it harder to see God's hand in our life.

- **"Pray the Room"**
    - ○ This is a form of imaginative prayer that combines intercession with waiting on and listening for God. The goal is to pray what the Spirit of Jesus is already wanting you to pray from deep within.
    - ○ Get to a quiet, distraction-free place if at all possible. Take 5-10 deep, slow breaths.
    - ○ Close your eyes and imagine yourself in a room with the Father or Jesus. Take a moment to visualize the room. If no specific room takes shape in your mind, use your memory of a room you love and experience God in.

- Ask the Spirit to bring into the room anyone or anything that he wants you to pray for. Wait and see what comes into your field of vision.

    - How do they look? Are they happy? Sad? Bruised? Tired? Scared? Lost? What else do you notice about their appearance or demeanor?

- Then, pray for that person. Make your intercession as specific as possible. You can pray whatever is on your heart for them, or ask the Spirit for further insight into what to pray for them. If you don't know what to pray, just hold them before God with love.

- Consider reaching out to that person to check in or offer a word of encouragement or sense of God's heart for them.

Reach Practice

Reading

Read chapters 4-5 of *Praying Like Monks, Living Like Fools* by Tyler Staton (pp. 69-114).

Podcast

Listen to episode 2 of the Prayer series from the Rule of Life podcast by Practicing the Way.

Exercise: Praying your own lament

Praying lament is a deeply personal experience. This exercise has been designed to help you connect with your own feelings and experiences so you can freely express them to God. Don't feel like you need to go deep if you're not ready. Remember, honesty is where the real power is with lament, so try not to filter your emotions and words.

Follow the QR code above to a video tutorial from Strahan Coleman that will guide you step by step, using prayer prompts.

Or you can follow the written tutorial on the following pages.

NOTES

01 **Become aware** — To start, make yourself comfortable and take a few deep breaths. Become aware of your surroundings, the sounds, the temperature, how your body is today. Open up to God.

02 **Focus on a feeling** — Let yourself feel your present emotional state, your difficult situations and griefs and losses. You may have a few in your life. See if you can bring your focus to one of those emotions or situations that you're currently feeling hurt or angry about.

03 **Sit with it** — Sit with that feeling, without judging it or telling yourself it's good or bad. Just notice how it feels. Can you locate it in your body? Your gut? Chest? Back? Shoulders? What is it like to hold that within you?

04 **Bring it to God** — Now, imagine holding it out in your hands as you stand before him, so you can both see it. Tell God exactly how you feel, without a filter, and allow God to feel what you feel in this moment, to acknowledge the pain and grief that exists. Be raw, honest, and vulnerable. Let God hear all that's in your heart. Remember, you're taking your pain to him, on a quest for deeper intimacy, not rebellion. And know that God can bear it, and that he knows what it's like to hurt. Hebrews 4v15 tells us that God sympathizes with us. Give God consent to sympathize with your lament.

05 **Express your desires and needs.** Plead with God to act, to change what is, to redeem or vindicate or heal or save or fight on your behalf. Wrestle with God if you feel the permission to do so.

06 **Give God your trust.** Then, let go. You might want to say, "Even though I feel [insert your emotion or lament], you are good and I trust you with it." Or "I trust you, help my lack of trust!" Or use the ending to Jesus's own prayer of lament, "Not my will, but yours be done."

07 **Be still** — For a few minutes, be still before God and allow him to respond. You may feel a lightness or a peace, you may see a picture or hear a word in your mind or imagination, or you might not. Notice how you feel after letting God hear your lament. Whatever happens, allow God the opportunity to meet you in this moment.

08 **Give thanks** — Finally, take a moment to thank God for being with you in this space. For listening, and for caring.

Reminder: Start with where you are. As an alternative to the tutorial above, you can simply pray one of the Psalms of Lament. Scholars argue approximately two-thirds of the 150 psalms are prayers of lament.

Here are a few we recommend to pray: Psalm 10, 13, 22, 42, 74, 77

Prayer Reflection

WEEK 02: TALKING WITH GOD

Before your next time together with the group for Week 03, take five to ten minutes to journal out your answers to the following three questions.

01   Did you find any of last week's exercises difficult?

02   Do you have any stories of answered or *un*-answered prayer?

03   What did you sense God doing in you as you prayed?

Note: As you write, be as specific as possible. While bullet points are just fine, if you write it out in narrative form, your brain will be able to process your insights in a more lasting way.

Listening to God

WEEK 03

Overview

There comes a point in our relationship to God where we desire not just to speak to him, but to listen. To hear his voice. As Jesus said in John 10v27, "My sheep listen to my voice; I know them, and they follow me." This is a Spirit-generated desire in the heart of a disciple of Jesus. In Luke 10v39, it was said of Jesus' disciple Mary that she "sat at the Lord's feet, listening to what he said." This is the primary posture of a disciple of Jesus: sitting at his feet and listening.

But how do we hear God's voice? He doesn't speak in the ways we're used to. Yet he speaks in a variety of ways. Ultimately through Jesus, then Scripture, circumstances, desire, prophesy, dreams, visions, the "still small voice," and more.

Learning to sift through all the "voices" in our head and to discern how God is speaking to us is a key task of discipleship. But learning to hear is just the beginning; learning to obey is the even greater task. Our intention must be to really listen to God, with a heart of loving surrender and trust.

In this week's exercises, we practice two ancient and time-tested ways of listening to God.

Practice

01   *Lectio Divina*

This is an ancient Latin phrase, first used by St. Benedict in the sixth century. It means "spiritual reading." It's a way of reading Scripture slowly and prayerfully, listening for God's word to you.

While you do not need to follow this four-step process, there are four movements to *Lectio Divina* that you may find helpful.

First, get somewhere quiet and as distraction-free as possible. Open your Bible and pick out a passage that's conducive to *Lectio* — a Psalm, a portion of the Gospels, or a section of an epistle (another word for letter, such as Romans, Ephesians, Philippians, etc.). Take a few deep breaths. Then:

- **Read** — A passage of your choice, slowly and prayerfully. Pay special attention to any words or phrases or ideas that jump out to you, or that move you emotionally or deeply resonate.

- **Reflect** — Reread the passage again, slowly. This time, pause over the word(s) or phrase(s) that were highlighted to you during your first reading. Meditate on them. Turn them over in your mind. Savor them.

- **Respond** — Pray your impressions back to God. You can use your own words or simply pray the text directly to God.

- **Rest** — Take a few minutes in silence to breathe deeply and rest in God's loving word to you.

Repeat this 3-5 times this coming week.

If you're doing this as a group, find somewhere quiet and distraction-free and read the four steps above out loud. Share your impressions with one another and pray them together to God.

02 Listening Prayer

First, get somewhere quiet and distraction-free. Then:

- **Breathe** — Take a minute or two to just breathe slowly and deeply, clearing your mind to receive God's word to you. You may want to simply pray, "Father" or "Jesus" or "Come Holy Spirit" as you inhale and exhale each breath.

- **Silence** — Ask God to silence the voice of the enemy in your mind, to clear the air around you, to shield and guard your imagination.

- **Ask the Spirit to speak to you**

- **Open your mind and heart to listen** — 1 Corinthians 6v19 tells us our body is a "temple of the Holy Spirit." The Spirit within you has direct access to your imagination. Wait quietly with a surrendered heart. He may come to you in a:

  - Word or phrase

  - Scripture

  - Thought

  - Metaphor

  - Picture in your mind

  - Short film, kind of a series of pictures in your mind

  - Feeling in your heart

  - Sensation in your body

If nothing comes, don't judge yourself, or God. Just give thanks for his love and try again later. Our job is to be present to God and to listen for his voice when he desires to speak to us.

Test whatever you "hear" against Scripture and in community.

Finally, if God's word to you was directional, obey. Go do what he said!

NOTES

Reach Practice

Reading

Read chapters 6-8 of *Praying Like Monks, Living Like Fools* by Tyler Staton (pp. 115-162).

Podcast

Listen to episode 3 of the Prayer series from the Rule of Life podcast by Practicing the Way.

Exercise: Praying the Examen

This exercise, the Examen, was developed by St. Ignatius of Loyola as a way of reviewing our day with God. St. Ignatius taught that God often speaks through our emotions, and that, by becoming aware of them, we may also become aware of the Spirit's movements in our own lives. He also encouraged others to talk to Jesus as a friend, sitting with and sharing our lives with him. The Examen was designed as a regular practice for the end of the day or week.

Follow the QR code above to a video tutorial from Strahan Coleman that will guide you step by step, using prayer prompts.

Or you can follow the written tutorial on the following pages.

NOTES

NOTES

01 **Become aware of God** — Review the day with the eyes of the Spirit, asking God for the light to see. It may seem rushed to you, a blur or chaotic. If you feel overwhelmed or struggle to focus, ask the Spirit to help you see and bring focus to your mind.

02 **Look back with gratitude** — As you explore your day, take note of moments where you can thank God for what's been. It may be as simple as noting the provision of food and waking in the comfort of your bed. Think about the people in your day and the connections made. Where was God in each relationship or conversation? Recall the little things about your day, simple everyday pleasures, and discover God among them.

03 **Notice your emotions** — Reflect on your feelings throughout the day. What do you notice? Without judging what you felt, did you feel anger? Contentment? Empathy? Happiness? Embarrassment? Trusting that God speaks through our emotions, what do you think God was saying amidst them?

04 **Pray from one piece of your day** — Allowing the Spirit to highlight one element of your day, be it positive or negative, ask him to speak to you about it. Consider it with him and allow it to lead you to prayer, whether it's gratitude, intercession, petition, repentance, or praise.

05 **Look ahead to tomorrow** — Finally, ask God to prepare your heart for tomorrow. Notice how you feel about it — anxious, excited, nervous, overwhelmed — and invite the Spirit to speak to those joys and concerns. Ask for clarity for the day ahead and for peace to approach it with confidence. Ask for wisdom, for hope, for discernment.

Prayer Reflection

WEEK 03: LISTENING TO GOD

Before your next time together with the group for Week 04, take five to ten minutes to journal out your answers to the following three questions.

01   What was your experience trying listening prayer?

02   Did you sense God saying anything to you this week?

03   As you sat with God, did the Spirit convict or comfort you?

Note: As you write, be as specific as possible. While bullet points are just fine, if you write it out in narrative form, your brain will be able to process your insights in a more lasting way.

Being with God

WEEK 04

Overview

We never mature beyond any of the four stages of prayer we are exploring in this Practice, but the further we progress in prayer, the more we desire to speak to God, to listen to God, and to just be with God.

As a general rule, you can gauge the intimacy in a relationship by how comfortable you are being alone together in the silence. Early on, relationships are full of words and activity. As you grow closer over time, there are still words and activity, but you also come to deeply enjoy just being with each other.

In the later stages of prayer, all human metaphors fall short, but the most ancient metaphor for this stage is marriage. There is a level of intimacy in marriage that is the intermingling of persons at the deepest level. It is wordless, yet it is a form of communication, and more, communion. Followers of Jesus have long considered this sacred love to be a picture of union with God.

This type of wordless prayer has come to be called "contemplation," based on 2 Corinthians 3v18. Its most basic meaning is to contemplate: to look, to gaze upon the beauty of God, receiving his love pouring out toward you in Christ and by the Spirit, and then giving your love back in return.

In our final week's exercises, we explore this way of being with God in love.

Practice

WEEK 04: BEING WITH GOD

We only have one simple exercise for you in our final week.

01 Begin your daily prayer rhythm with silence and a breath prayer

The seventh century monk St. John Climacus gave this advice on contemplation: "Let the memory of Jesus combine with your breath." Contemplatives have long used the God-ordained process of breathing to attune to the breath/spirit/*pnuema* of God within the "temple" of our body. God has designed deep, slow breathing to calm your body's nervous system and center your mind. That makes breathing an especially helpful pathway to contemplative prayer.

Contemplative prayer is difficult because our mind is so distraction-prone, but the basic steps are simple.

- Find a quiet, distraction-free place to pray.

- Get seated comfortably, but where you can breathe properly and not slouch. We recommend either a dining chair with your feet on the floor and your back straight and shoulders upright, or sitting cross-legged directly on the floor, with a pillow or cushion under your backside to help with blood circulation. Not on a couch.

- Breathe slowly (five seconds on the inhale, then five on the exhale) from your belly. Relax. Become present to your body. And to the moment. Then, open your mind to God.

- You may just want to remain here, in loving attention to the Trinity.

Remember: You're not trying to pray words here. It's your heart to God's heart; this prayer is will to will, love to love.

- Or you may want to combine a prayer word to your breath. A prayer word is simply a word or phrase that you use to keep your attention fixed on God.
    - Many use "Father" or "Abba" or "Jesus"
    - Others use a phrase from Scripture like "The Lord is my shepherd" (on the inhale), "I lack nothing" (on the exhale).
    - The Eastern church uses the Jesus Prayer: "Lord Jesus Christ" (on the inhale), "have mercy on me" (on the exhale).
    - You can also use your own phrase, like, "In you I live" (on the inhale), and "In you I delight" (on the exhale).
    - There's no "right" prayer word. It's just a tool to keep your wandering mind focused on God's presence within you.

- When distractions come, just gently set them aside the moment you realize your mind has wandered and come back to your breathing and prayer word. And they will come, way more than you think or want! That's okay. It doesn't mean you're bad at contemplative prayer; it means you're human.

Remain in God, receiving his love and giving yours back in turn. In the beginning, 1-2 minutes of this is a huge success, and 5-10 minutes is a home run.

Reach Practice

Reading

Read chapters 9-10 of *Praying Like Monks, Living Like Fools* by Tyler Staton (pp. 163-216)

Podcast

Listen to episode 4 of the Prayer series from the Rule of Life podcast by Practicing the Way.

Exercise: Beholding Prayer (The Window of the Soul)

This exercise — The Window of the Soul — is one way to practice beholding (or contemplative prayer). What's important is that we bring all of ourselves to God and allow him to be present to us with compassion, kindness, and love. Setting our eyes on the God that is, and not the one we may assume or fear. It can take practice to become comfortable with this kind of prayer, so don't worry if you don't fully connect the first time. The most important part is our being lovingly available to God.

Follow the QR code above to a video tutorial from Strahan Coleman that will guide you step by step, using prayer prompts.

Or you can follow the written tutorial on the following pages.

NOTES

NOTES

01 **Become aware** — Make yourself comfortable and take a few deep breaths. Become aware of your surroundings — the sounds, the temperature, etc. How does your body feel today? Heavy, light, sore, calm? Reconnecting with ourselves helps bring all of us to God in prayer.

02 **Sink into your heart** — Try and focus on where you feel the deepest within your body. It may be in your heart, your chest, or your belly. If you're not sure, try to imagine there is an elevator that descends down from your head, through your neck, past your collar bone and into your heart. Place those thoughts in the elevator and send them down into your heart. Don't deny them or try to get rid of them, just allow them to sink into your heart's center as you pray.

03 **Open yourself up to God** — While you're in that space, begin to open yourself up to God. If it's helpful, imagine that there are outward opening French doors within you, where your soul feels most present. As you picture them, imagine opening those doors to God and offering him every part of who you are. The good, the not good, the celebrated, and the vulnerable or ashamed. Imagine yourself having no part of you left hidden by choice from God. All is available to be seen.

04 **Look to God** — As you bring your whole self to him, look toward him. You might imagine Jesus' face, or you may simply look toward his loving presence. In John 15v9, Jesus said, "As the Father has loved me, so I have loved you." Allow yourself to see God gazing upon you with love, openness, compassion, and joy. Give him consent to reveal that love toward you personally. Imagine his gaze pouring through the doorway to your soul.

05 **Sit with God** — Without agenda, allow him to be however he longs to be with you. You may feel or see something beautiful. If not, this time is just as important. Let yourself just be open to God in whatever way today demands, allowing him to be with you. Notice how it feels to be fully seen by God and to be fully open toward him.

06 **Return your awareness** — As you finish your time together, take a moment to thank God for his love and for being present to you. Then, slowly come back into awareness of the sounds and sensations of the room around you.

Note: For each step, take a minute or two to sit and abide in the process.

Prayer Reflection

WEEK 04: BEING WITH GOD

As you come to the end of this Practice, take five to ten minutes to journal out your answers to the following three questions.

01   How did the Beholding Prayer excercise go for you?

02   How did you handle distraction when you prayed?

03   How and where have you sensed God's *with*-ness in your life?

Note: As you write, be as specific as possible. While bullet points are just fine, if you write it out in narrative form, your brain will be able to process your insights in a more lasting way.

NOTES

Keep Going

Continue the Journey

You are *not* going to explore the vast territory of prayer in four weeks. This Practice is only designed to get you moving on a lifelong journey. The daily prayer rhythm you've been practicing is meant to be integrated into your Rule of Life and become the baseline for your life with God. But prayer is a journey in which we never "arrive," and there is always more.

Where you go from here is entirely up to you, but if you decide to integrate a daily prayer rhythm into your life, here's a list of next steps to continue your Practice.

Recommend Reading

01 *Beholding* by Strahan Coleman

02 *Armchair Mystic* by Mark E. Thibodeaux

03 *A Praying Life* by Paul E. Miller

04 *God on Mute* by Pete Greig

05 *Hearing God* by Dallas Willard

06 *Domestic Monastery* by Ronald Rolheiser

Recommended exercises

01   Practice Sabbath

Most of us are simply too busy to pray. Sabbath is one of the most important disciplines for the spiritual life in our day, because it opens up time and space in our overcrowded lives to find our life in God. The practice of Sabbath is like a container for so many other practices.

The Sabbath Practice is available at practicingtheway.org/sabbath, but here are a few small steps to get started.

- Choose a day to Sabbath (or if a full 24 hours is too much, start with a half day or a few hours after church).

- Begin your Sabbath with some kind of small ritual to transition into Sabbath time — like lighting a candle, reading a psalm, or eating a meal with family or friends.

- Spend your Sabbath ceasing from all work, chores, buying, selling, and entertainment. In their place, give yourself to rest, delight, and worship.

- Run the Sabbath Practice, listen to the Rule of Life podcast Series One: Sabbath, and/or read a book about the Sabbath to continue to learn more about this ancient discipline for emotional health and spiritual life.

02   Go on retreat

Find a monastery, retreat center, rural hotel, or vacation home and go away for an extended time of quiet, rest, Sabbath, and prayer. If going away isn't feasible in this season, eight hours is a great start and can expand over time. Two to three days would be harder, but deeply impactful and worth working your way up to over the course of a few retreats.

The longer we give ourselves to solitude, silence, and stillness, the more space it opens up in us for healing and renewal in God.

03 Continue to develop a daily prayer rhythm

We need to develop a rich life with God in our ordinary life, not just on retreat or special occasions. Our daily rhythms of prayer are absolutely essential to our discipleship. The best place to start is by developing and fine-tuning your daily prayer rhythm, or what ancient Christians called the "Daily Office".

Once you've firmly established a daily prayer habit each morning (or whenever you decide is best for you to pray), begin to slowly expand.

Choose a second time and place to pause for another moment of daily prayer. If you pray in the morning, try stopping again after work and before dinner (when you're not too tired) or just before bed (if you're more of a night person). Or try praying on your lunch break or during a break in your daily routine of work, school, or caregiving. You may want to use your body differently: If you sit for morning prayer, try going on a walk or standing or kneeling.

Experiment with different types of prayer that meet different needs, like petition and intercession midday and the Examen at night (or whatever you discern is best).

When you get busy and fall out of your rhythm, don't judge yourself or feel bad; it's very normal. Just begin again.

Remember: The end goal is not to pray X number of times a day. It's to rearrange your daily life so you are experiencing deep joy, peace, and gratitude in your everyday life with God.

Appendix: Prayers

St. Francis of Assisi's "Make Me an Instrument of Your Peace"

Lord, make me an instrument of your peace.
Where there is hatred, let me sow love;
where there is injury, pardon;
where there is doubt, faith;
where there is despair, hope;
where there is darkness, light;
and where there is sadness, joy.

O Divine Master, grant that I may not so much seek
to be consoled as to console;
to be understood as to understand;
to be loved as to love.
For it is in giving that we receive;
it is in pardoning that we are pardoned;
and it is in dying that we are born to eternal life.
Amen.

"The Serenity Prayer"*

God grant me the serenity
To accept the things I cannot change;
Courage to change the things I can;
And wisdom to know the difference.
Living one day at a time;
Enjoying one moment at a time;
Accepting hardships as the pathway to peace;
Taking, as He did, this sinful world
As it is, not as I would have it;
Trusting that He will make all things right If I surrender to His Will;
So that I may be reasonably happy in this life
And supremely happy with Him
Forever and ever in the next.
Amen.

*Likely composed by the theologian Reinhold Niebuhr, but popularized by
Alcoholics Anonymous

St. Teresa of Ávila's "Guidance Prayer"

Lord,

grant that I may always allow myself to be guided by You,

always follow Your plans,

and perfectly accomplish Your Holy Will.

Grant that in all things, great and small,

today and all the days of my life,

I may do whatever You require of me.

Help me respond to the slightest prompting of Your Grace,

so that I may be Your trustworthy instrument for Your honor.

May Your Will be done in time and in eternity by me,

in me, and through me.

Amen.

St. Teresa of Ávila's "Bookmark Prayer"*

Let nothing disturb you;

Let nothing frighten you.

All things are passing.

God never changes.

Patience obtains all things.

Nothing is wanting to him who possesses God.

God alone suffices.

*Named "Bookmark Prayer" because it was found on a handwritten bookmark upon her death.

St. Patrick's "Breastplate Prayer"

I arise today
Through a mighty strength, the invocation of the Trinity,
Through belief in the Threeness,
Through confession of the Oneness
of the Creator of creation.
I arise today
Through the strength of Christ's birth with His baptism,
Through the strength of His crucifixion with His burial,
Through the strength of His resurrection with His ascension,
Through the strength of His descent for the judgment of doom.
I arise today
Through the strength of the love of cherubim,
In the obedience of angels,
In the service of archangels,
In the hope of resurrection to meet with reward,
In the prayers of patriarchs,
In the predictions of prophets,
In the preaching of apostles,
In the faith of confessors,
In the innocence of holy virgins,
In the deeds of righteous men.
I arise today, through
The strength of heaven,
The light of the sun,
The radiance of the moon,
The splendor of fire,
The speed of lightning,
The swiftness of wind,
The depth of the sea,
The stability of the earth,
The firmness of rock.
I arise today, through
God's strength to pilot me,
God's might to uphold me,
God's wisdom to guide me,

God's eye to look before me,
God's ear to hear me,
God's word to speak for me,
God's hand to guard me,
God's shield to protect me,
God's host to save me
From snares of devils,
From temptation of vices,
From everyone who shall wish me ill,
afar and near.
I summon today
All these powers between me and those evils,
Against every cruel and merciless power
that may oppose my body and soul,
Against incantations of false prophets,
Against black laws of pagandom,
Against false laws of heretics,
Against craft of idolatry,
Against spells of witches and smiths and wizards,
Against every knowledge that corrupts man's body and soul;
Christ to shield me today
Against poison, against burning,
Against drowning, against wounding,
So that there may come to me an abundance of reward.
Christ with me,
Christ before me,
Christ behind me,
Christ in me,
Christ beneath me,
Christ above me,
Christ on my right,
Christ on my left,
Christ when I lie down,
Christ when I sit down,
Christ when I arise,

Christ in the heart of every man who thinks of me,
Christ in the mouth of everyone who speaks of me,
Christ in every eye that sees me,
Christ in every ear that hears me.
I arise today
Through a mighty strength, the invocation of the Trinity,
Through belief in the Threeness,
Through confession of the Oneness
of the Creator of creation.

James K. Baxter's "Song to the Lord God"

Lord God, you are above and beyond all things,
Your nature is to love,
You put us in the furnace of the world
To learn to love you and love one another.

Father, we sing to you in the furnace
Like the three Jewish children.
The hope and the doom of the love of friends
Is eating up the marrow of our bones.

Lord Christ, you are the house in whom we live,
The house in which we share the cup of peace,
The house of your body that was broken on the cross,
The house you have built for us beyond the stars.

Lord, Holy Spirit, beyond, within, above,
Beneath all things, you give us life.
Blaze in our hearts, you who are Love himself,
Till we shine like the noonday sun.

Lord God, we are the little children,
The feeble ones of the world.
Carry us for ever in your breast, Lord God,
Give us the power by love to be your holy ones.

MORNING PRAYER

By Strahan Coleman, from *Prayer Vol. 02*

As the dawning light ascends, God,
  so do I to you,
    so do I in you,
    to the melody of your love.
Today is yours, Father,
  and as with every day,
    You have made it ours.
So may my steps be as Your steps,
  my words be as Your words,
    and my heart be as Your heart,
  until the dusk arrives
to beckon me to rest once more.

MIDDAY PRAYER

From *The New Zealand Prayer Book*

Let us be at peace within ourselves.

Silence

Let us accept that we are profoundly loved
and need never be afraid.

Silence

Let us be aware of the source of being
that is common to us all
and to all living creatures.

Silence

Let us be filled with the presence of the great compassion
towards ourselves and towards all living beings.

Silence

Realizing that we are all nourished
from the same source of life,
may we so live that others be not deprived
of air, food, water, shelter, or the chance to live.

Silence

Let us pray that we ourselves cease to be
a cause of suffering to one another.

Silence

With humility let us pray for the establishment
of peace in our hearts and on earth.

Silence

EVENING PRAYERS

"Compline Prayer"

From *The Book of Common Prayer*

Keep watch, dear Lord, with those who work, or watch, or weep this night, and give your angels charge over those who sleep. Tend the sick, Lord Christ; give rest to the weary, bless the dying, soothe the suffering, pity the afflicted, shield the joyous; and all for your love's sake. Amen.

"Night Prayer"

From *He Karakia Mihinare o Aotearoa/A New Zealand Prayer Book*

Lord,
it is night.

The night is for stillness.
Let us be still in the presence of God.
It is night after a long day.
What has been done has been done;
what has not been done has not been done;
let it be.

The night is dark.
Let our fears of the darkness of the world and of our own lives
rest in you.

The night is quiet.
Let the quietness of your peace enfold us,
all dear to us,
and all who have no peace.

The night heralds the dawn.
Let us look expectantly to a new day,
new joys,
new possibilities.

In your name we pray.
Amen.

By Strahan Coleman, from *Prayer Vol. 02*

We are with ourselves here in the dark, Father,
 aware of our vulnerabilities,
  our needs and mortal limitations.
All we have done today is now left to rest in You,
 or grow in You,
  depending on Your will.
We have done all we could,
 yet perhaps not all we should,
  we trust You now as always, God,
  with both.

Meet us as we sleep, so our souls —
 our hearts — will wake with new
  energy for greater love.
You will never leave us,
 not in the day,
  and now not in the night.
We trust in You with all our
 greatest love and hope.